CW00338962

*It's the Gospel Truth!*

# It's The Gospel Truth!

*Weird and Wonderful Church Stories*

## Colin Blakely

Marshall Pickering
*An Imprint of* HarperCollins*Publishers*

Marshall Pickering is an Imprint of
HarperCollins*Religious*
Part of HarperCollins*Publishers*
77–85 Fulham Palace Road
London W6 8JB

First published in Great Britain
in 1998 by Marshall Pickering

10 9 8 7 6 5 4 3 2 1

A catalogue record for this book is
available from the British Library

ISBN 0 551 03131 X

Text illustrations by Taffy Davies

Printed and bound in Great Britain by
MacKays of Chatham plc

To Libby

# *Contents*

# *Preface*

In the ancient world Herodotus became known as the Father of History, for he scoured the world to verify the legends he had heard. Only those that could be substantiated made it into his Histories. I claim no similar authentication. I have compiled here a collection of such stories, known in the trade as 'urban myths', because they largely cannot be verified and while some are true (and I know because my wife features in one) many of the others have been doing the rounds since Adam was a boy. It would be impossible to prove their truth and on looking at these stories one gets the distinct impression that they probably never happened, but someone, somewhere, desperately wished they did.

Many of us will remember the story that apparently took place in Harrods when a young woman wanted to buy a necklace with a cross pendant. The counter clerk inquired of her, the now famous question: 'Would you like a plain one or one with a little man on it?' (My editor swears she actually heard this conversation once, though it wasn't in Harrods...)

It was the Rev Bryan Barrowdale who said (or so I am told): 'Religion needs to be joked about more than anything else. Only God is to be taken with unreserved seriousness.' As the Church has had to endure endless claims about the key elements of the Christian story being no more than 'myths', I am pleased to present some stories that can undoubtedly fall into this category. These myths are about the Church and I hope that they will bring a smile to your face.

Many of these stories take on a life of their own. When I first suggested this collection to my editor, she commented that she recognized some of the stories, believing that they had happened to 'a friend of a friend'. No doubt you will too. Many of these incidents have grown legs over time and the stories have developed and mutated and have seeped into our collective consciousness. Some of them were perhaps stories that were intended once to make a moral point, but on reflection it is perhaps more likely that they were intended to fulfil the 'tall poppy' syndrome – seeing the mighty being cut down to size.

There are undoubtedly many more of these stories in circulation than are recounted here. I am grateful to readers of the *Church of England Newspaper* who have been quick to recount stories they know of (and even feature in) and I am also grateful to those friends who have cheerfully recounted how friends of theirs (or friends of friends of theirs) have had their come-uppance. Grateful thanks are also due to Taffy for his excellent cartoons which enhance this book. If you have any stories that come under the category of urban myth, I would be more than pleased to receive them.

**CHAPTER 1**

# Clerical Errors

## Foam Home

A clergy wife answered the door of their large, rambling vicarage one morning to find two young lads from a cavity wall insulation firm who had come to help them curb their winter heating bills.

As the lady was due at a parish coffee morning in the village, she explained to the lads that they should start their work upstairs, and pointed to the master bedroom – thinking to herself that the job would be completed by the time she returned, leaving the room clear for her to have her afternoon nap.

Suitably instructed, the young men unloaded their equipment and set to work in the rather grand bedroom. They manhandled the drums of insulating foam up the stairs and, having covered the bedroom with sheets, they began the work of insulating the cavities. Having drilled a hole in the wall, one of the pair then began the lengthy process of injecting the quick-drying foam, while the other took advantage of the double bed to read his daily tabloid.

All was going well, and the first drum was soon used up. Although this was surprising, they hooked up a second drum and began injecting that too. A short while later that drum was emptied too. Finally, one of the workmen realized that something was wrong. On inspecting the wall closely, they realized that they had, in fact, injected the wrong wall.

Running next door, they found, to their horror, that they had been spraying the sticky yellow foam, not into an outer wall, but into the next door bedroom.

## Nativity Nightmare

A young clergy couple were proud of their two small children, and were particularly pleased when the eldest made her acting debut at the parish nativity play one year.

The couple called all of the relatives they could muster to the service at which their child would appear as the Virgin Mary. All went well in the preparations, with costumes designed accurately and lines learnt off by heart.

When the day of the big performance arrived, it was not only the couple who were listening eagerly to the play – the church was packed.

Mary and Joseph arrived at the inn and asked if they could have a room for the night. The innkeeper – a seven-year-old – decided that he knew the tale better and told the infant couple: 'You can come in, Mary, but I haven't got room for your husband.'

After an awkward giggle from the congregation the actors resumed their composure and the play continued.

The next scene featured the holy couple after the birth with the shepherds and the wise men, the latter of whom inquired of Mary: 'And what will you call the child?'

Her moment had approached. Her parents were watching; her father was recording the moment on his video camera and he caught, for posterity, her reply: 'I want to call her Julia.'

## Healing Hands

A clergyman in the north had been suffering for some time with back problems. Everything he tried had only limited success and despite all sorts of treatment and physiotherapy he was still in severe pain.

One of his parishioners suggested that he visit a Chinese acupuncturist, and having such a personal recommendation he decided that it would not be incompatible with his Christian faith to try out this form of alternative therapy.

In the event, the Chinese expert seemed to offer little more than an unusual form of physio, but remarkably the treatment worked. The clergyman found that his back was free of pain and he didn't even have to endure pins being stuck in his person.

The treatment was rather expensive for his clergy stipend, but the results were such that he counted it more than worth the price. So much so that he continued the treatment for several weeks – just to make sure that the pain did not return.

One morning, as he was sitting in the waiting room, he was joined by a rather old Chinese gentleman. He decided to inquire whether the service provided here was the same genuine traditional Chinese treatment as 'back in the old country'.

'Oh yes, much the same,' said the wizened old man. 'This doctor is very good. But for the life of me, I can't understand why he has a certificate up on his wall saying that he is licensed to sell fish in Hong Kong harbour.'

## Taking Note

A clergyman was once asked if he would appear in court as a character witness for a member of his congregation who was accused in an indecent assault case.

His testimony undoubtedly helped the accused man and the vicar stayed on to listen to the prosecution's case. The counsel gently asked the woman what had happened and she dutifully reported her side. When the defence came to question her she was asked what the accused had said to her. She blushed and said it was too embarrassing to repeat. The judge intervened and stressed the importance of finding out exactly what had been said. He suggested that she write it down, and she agreed.

Her words were written down and passed to the judge. He then asked a court official to pass the piece of paper to the jury, so that they could read it for themselves.

At the back of the jury was a man who had dozed off in the heat of the afternoon. The woman juror sitting next to him received the note, read it and passed it to him. As he was dozing, she had to nudge him and he sat upright and received the note. He read it, blushed and put it into his pocket.

The judge called to him to return the note, to which he responded: 'This is a private matter, m'lud, between this juror and myself.'

## Caught Short

A young clergyman, before beginning his training for the ministry, was advised to get some experience in industry. He discovered that in order to meet this demand he could simply spend a summer working on a building site.

He rather enjoyed this experience, and found it illuminating to discover the range of attitudes held by his fellow workmates.

One day, finding himself caught short after enjoying a spicy curry the night before, he decided to take advantage of the facilities at the house he was building; so he made his way to the smallest room in the house and enjoyed the relief.

Afterwards, he was perplexed to find that there was no toilet paper. No problem, he thought to himself, – I'll use this newspaper I have here. He used the paper, and turned to flush the toilet – only to discover that the toilet was not yet connected to the plumbing system.

# Food for Thought

The ladies of the parish were rather pleased with their new vicar, but they were somewhat dismayed that he was so shy. Many clergy share this attribute and it can be quite becoming, but this man's shyness was quite painful. He had won several friends with his superb Bible teaching skills and his self-deprecating sense of humour, but all attempts to put him at ease in company proved futile.

One day, a lady in the congregation invited him to lunch, at which she served a fish dish. The clergyman approached the table and sat down.

At this point he felt his sense of unease return. Should he offer to say grace or should he say it privately? He decided to say it privately and bent his head and closed his eyes.

His hostess, spying his perplexed demeanour, tried to make him feel more relaxed, announcing: 'It's quite, quite fresh, Vicar. Quite fresh. No need to worry on that account!'

# Digging for Victory

A vicar was having trouble with the plumbing in his house, and was frustrated by the diocesan red tape which stated that before any work could be carried out it would have to be inspected by the Archdeacon and the diocesan surveyor – and that was before they even considered calling in a plumber!

The vicar eventually decided that he could save the parish quite a lot of money by carrying out the repair himself. Although he was not a plumber, he knew enough about it to be confident that he could sort out such a minor problem.

So he set to work. The first problem was that the leak appeared to be outside the house. That made things a little more difficult. Undeterred, however, he borrowed his son's metal detector to locate the pipe so that he could mend it.

Armed with his new tool he set out and instantly found a positive signal just outside the front door of the vicarage. With the help of a pick-axe he dug up the path and went quite a way down but there was no sign of any piping.

He gave up on that hole and decided to try again. Almost immediately he got another signal from the metal detector, quite close to where he had been digging, so he got out the pick-axe and started again. The story was the same again – he got a signal from the detector but when he dug a hole, there was no metal to be found.

He had dug eight holes, and worked up quite a sweat in the process when he suddenly realized his error – the metal detector had been activated not by piping underground, but by the steel toe-caps in his boots.

## Something for the Weekend

A single, young curate was settling in to the new parish, and was very keen to make himself as popular as he could with the parishioners. Having volunteered to help out with the youth club one night, he arrived at the church hall a little early.

As he did, he saw one of the mothers dropping off her children. Taking the opportunity to chat, he was informed that she had been on a health education course that day, where the subject had been sex. At the class, all of the students had been given condoms. She joked about this to the curate and pulled a handful out of her pocket. 'Here you are,' she said, 'you can have these ones – I've still got plenty left.' Taken aback by the offer, he sheepishly put them in his pocket and they finished chatting.

Gathering the youth group together, he unlocked the hall and began to get things ready for the evening session. Once the seats were out and the kettle was put on he, together with the other helpers, began to organize the meeting. The curate reached for his jacket and pulled out his notes from his pocket, bringing with them the selection of condoms he had been given earlier.

His fellow helpers saw them and waited expectantly for the explanation...

## A Timely Question

Many years ago a bishop was making an official visit to New York. This was in the early days of aeroplanes and he made headlines being the first Anglican bishop to cross the Atlantic by air.

His arrival in the Big Apple led to frenzied interest from the media. In fact, as soon as he landed he found that he was surrounded by press reporters and photographers who were hot on the trail of what they regarded as a scoop.

One of the reporters, dressed in regulation raincoat and trilby, called out his question to the bishop: 'Hey bishop, will you be visiting any night-clubs while you are in New York?'

The befuddled bishop, taken aback by the line of questioning, replied: 'Are there any night-clubs in New York?'

The questioning continued on other, more ecclesiastical matters and, satisfied with their photo opportunity, the bishop and the press pack parted company.

The next morning the bishop was horrified to see the front pages of the papers, with his photograph next to the banner headline: 'Bishop's first question in USA – "Are there any night-clubs in New York?" '

## Car-ried Away

A vicar in the West Country was scanning the classified adverts section of his local newspaper when he saw what he believed to be a misprint: 'Porsche for sale, excellent condition, £50.00'. No one could sell a high performance car for such an amount, he reasoned, wondering if it was a joke or a misprint. He decided to call the number, thinking that even if the price was £5000 it would still be a bargain and one he could afford on his clergy stipend.

A few hours later he found himself outside a rather posh house looking at a beautiful car. The owner, a

11

middle-aged lady who was dressed in expensive clothes, confirmed that the price was indeed only £50. She suggested that he take a test drive.

After a spin around the block, the man could not believe his luck and with a sense of deep joy passed over the requested £50.

After the formal business was completed the man set out for home in his new car. But before he left he asked the woman, 'Tell me how you can afford to sell this car for just £50.'

The woman told him her husband had run off with his secretary the week before and had contacted her with an order to sell the house and the car and to send him the money.

'By the way, how much would you give me for the house?' she asked.

## Decisions, Decisions

A bishop was entertaining two new curates in his diocese. One was a very stern and imposing man who seemed to wear a permanent look of disapproval. The other was a timid young man, just out of theological college and very eager to please his bishop.

The bishop offered the timid young curate a glass of sherry, which the man gratefully accepted, despite the fact that he wasn't really very fond of sherry.

When the bishop offered the stern curate a glass, the curate roared: 'Intoxicating liquor is the very nose-droppings of the devil. I would rather commit adultery than drink of your sherry.'

The bishop, not surprisingly, was taken aback at this reaction, but he was stunned when the timid curate piped up, offering back his still unsipped glass, 'Oh, I didn't realize there was a choice.'

# House Guest

A curate had settled into his new parish, and was enjoying the lovely house the parish had provided. Situated right next to the church, it was also the home to the parish office.

One weekend he invited an old college friend over, and she decided to stay overnight, sleeping on the sofa. Fearing the questioning he would face, he suggested that the best policy would be for her to leave first thing in the morning. As he would be taking the 8 o'clock service, he explained to her how to leave the premises without being seen.

So the next morning the young, attractive girl rose early and packed her belongings. She then set off and diligently closed the door behind her. As it slammed shut she realized to her horror that the curate had mortice-locked the front door and she was now trapped in the vestibule, with no way out.

Her hopes of a quiet escape were dashed when the church secretary came to her aid and the curate unwittingly provided weeks of gossip...

# Man's Best Friend

A new vicar was enjoying the first few weeks in his new
parish. As part of the process of familiarizing himself
with the area he decided to combine his fact-finding with
visiting parish members.

Having sought out the lists of people to visit he set
off. The first few visits went well, but his heart sank as
he approached the next house on his visit, for sitting
outside the front door was a Rottweiler. Summoning all
his courage he decided that he would go ahead anyway.
He approached the door and the dog looked at him but
made no move.

After knocking on the door, the lady of the house
appeared and invited the vicar in. The dog got up and
followed him into the house.

The visit went well, with the dog sitting on the carpet
eyeing the clergyman with intent. A few minutes, and a
cup of tea later, the dog got up and walked over to the
settee, where it cocked its leg and did its business. The
vicar was shocked that the family allowed it to behave
in this way, but he was more taken aback that no one
in the family said anything. Instead, the conversation
moved on.

After a decent interval the vicar made his excuses and
left. As he departed, the father of the house called to him.
'Aren't you going to take your dog with you?'

# Phone Pest

A clergyman was about to make a long train journey and as he boarded the train he was pleased to see there were many free seats. He chose a seat in the direction of travel, with a table. He thought this would be a good opportunity to catch up on some paperwork.

But the train soon proved to be rather busier than he anticipated and far from having the group of four seats to himself, he found himself facing a grandmother and grandson who had brought a picnic with them.

To add to the horror he was soon joined by a young, upwardly mobile gentleman who sat next to him. This was not a discreet businessman, he noticed, but rather a brash and somewhat loud entrepreneur.

However, the clergyman got down to his paperwork as the train pulled out of the station.

As the train got up speed the man sitting next to the clergyman got out a mobile phone and proceeded to call up his business associates, noisily talking about huge business deals he was pulling off, instructing his broker to 'buy' or 'sell' and to call up hotels ordering expensive meals to be prepared for his arrival.

The clergyman gave up all hope of completing any work, and decided to try to get some sleep. He was awakened a few minutes later by a commotion going on around him. One of the other passengers had taken ill, and the young entrepreneur was asked for the use of his mobile phone to alert the emergency services.

Everyone, including the clergyman felt a strange sense of satisfaction when the man admitted his phone was in fact a fake.

# Garden Bloomer

The new curate had been asked to take a wedding on the day of the vicarage garden party being held next door to the church.

Unfortunately, he had not been told that the vestry was being used by the judo team, who were putting on a show as part of the day.

All had gone well until the happy couple were led to the vestry for the signing of the register. As the curate opened the door, the bride was presented with the sight of a room full of naked men.

The curate hastily closed the door and called for the men to disperse. They decided to take up their clothes and leave by the back entrance. As the men cleared out of the vestry, in various stages of undress, they found themselves in the middle of the garden party.

# Hair-Raising Experience

An elderly clergyman, deciding to try out a new hair-dresser, went to a unisex salon instead of his regular barber. He was impressed by the service on offer – he was offered a cup of coffee while he was waiting, and the stylist chatted to him about what sort of haircut and style he was looking for. This was a long way from his regular barber, who only offered a number 1, 2, 3 or 4.

When he was ready for the chop, he was pleasantly surprised to find that a girl took him to have his hair washed. Feeling like he was in the lap of luxury, the vast sums his wife spent on hair-dos finally made sense.

The girl finished washing and conditioning his hair and took him into the salon. She sat him down in front of a mirror and put a gown over him. 'The stylist will be with you in a minute,' she said, and went off.

A few minutes later the stylist duly arrived and began cutting the reverend's hair. She was perplexed, however, to note that the old man was staring at her in a strange way, and her worries were magnified when she saw his hands moving in a suspicious manner under the gown.

Furious, she slapped him on the head, shouted 'pervert' and stormed off.

When she struck him, she managed to knock the frail old man off the seat. However, her conscience got the better of her and she went back to help him up. As she did so, she noticed that he had been cleaning his spectacles under the gown.

# Six Is a Crowd

A new curate was settling into his new church, and was looking forward to his marriage the following year. His bride-to-be lived a long way away and they only saw each other occasionally, because she worked, and when she was free at weekends, the curate was busy with parish duties.

This did not deter the curate, and he decided to make the most of the time to buy things for their new marital home. He spent a lot of money and when his bride eventually moved in, she was pleased to see the gifts he had bought for her.

She noticed that he had bought many things for the kitchen and dining room. However, although she counted

12 pieces of most things, she wondered why her new husband had only bought six steak knives.

'Well, if we ever can afford steak, we won't be having any more than six people,' he told her.

# Life Preserver

The wife of a vicar in the west country was constantly bemused by her husband's preoccupation with DIY. Sometimes she felt that the family home was like the laboratory of some mad scientist, because there was so much work going on.

Intricate lighting systems and remote control devices had made their home look like something Heath Robinson could have devised, but most of his efforts weren't much good.

One day his wife was returning from a shopping trip when she spotted him through the kitchen window. She was shocked to see that he had his hand on the kettle and was shaking uncontrollably.

She ran indoors thinking one of his experiments had gone badly wrong, and picked up the first thing that came to hand – their child's baseball bat. She grabbed it and hit her husband on the chest to try to break his link with the electricity supply and she whacked him so hard he landed on the floor with serious bruising to the chest.

It turned out he had been making a cup of tea while dancing to some music on his personal stereo.

## Running On Empty

It was one of those hot summer days when you can see
the heat haze rise from the ground. And it was on a day
such as this that a vicar was driving in the country. His
journey came to an abrupt end, however, when he ran
out of petrol.

While this was perplexing, it did not upset him too
much, as he knew he would enjoy a walk in the country-
side on such a pleasant day. So, gathering his things
together, he set off for the nearest village, slightly concerned that he did not have a spare petrol can. No matter,
he thought to himself, the garage is bound to have one
I can borrow.

A short while later he arrived in the village and found
the petrol station. He explained his predicament to the

garage attendant, who explained that he did not have any spare containers. He suggested the vicar look at the back of the petrol station to see if he could find any container that would meet his purpose.

After a few minutes' searching the vicar could only find an old porcelain potty. He mused that while it might not be ideal it would do.

He filled it with unleaded petrol and returned to his car. At first he found it rather awkward to get the petrol from the potty to the tank, but he soon managed to find an angle that worked.

As he was standing there pouring the petrol in, a car pulled up beside him. A rather posh lady looked and called out, 'I wish I had your faith, Vicar.'

## Dressed For Success?

A young clergyman had spent the weekend speaking at a conference and was returning to his home parish, where he was looking forward to a visit from the diocesan bishop.

He had spent the weekend lounging around the conference centre and planned to return home early to change into smarter clothes.

However, the train on which he was travelling was held up and consequently he returned to his home town rather late. Too late, he feared, to return home to the vicarage before meeting the bishop at the church.

As he left the railway station he was in something of a panic – the clothes he was wearing were rather crumpled to say the least. However, as he made his way hurriedly down the road, he spotted a sign that read 'Trousers pressed'.

Thinking on his feet, he thought that he could take advantage of this service. He ran into the shop. As there was no one behind the counter, he thought he would save time by taking his trousers off. No problem, he reasoned, he was wearing a presentable pair of boxer shorts underneath.

The shop assistant then returned and looked at him in disbelief. 'What do you think you are doing?' she demanded.

Pointing to the sign in the window he said: 'I'd like these trousers pressed, please.'

The shop assistant put him right: 'We don't press trousers, we paint signs.'

## Lost For Words

A new incumbent was enjoying his first few months in his parish, and he took every opportunity to meet his new flock. Rather than drive around the village, he decided to walk everywhere, believing that this would allow him to meet the locals much quicker.

One day, soon after Christmas, he went to collect his eight-year-old son who was playing with a friend. Clutching his favourite toy, a small soft cuddly fox, the son took his father's hand for the short walk home.

On the way the father decided to teach his son about alliteration. 'The fiery fox frightened a fire-fly,' he said.

His son was slightly impressed with this, but his father was now in his stride. 'The fierce fox as quick as a flash fled through a forest then fell on his face.'

His son moaned: 'Oh Dad!'

But the father was not deterred. As they approached the village shops, he continued his creative flush. 'Flash the fox fed up with fighting, frightening and fleeing flew off as fast as...'

His son interrupted, as they approached some villagers: 'Oh Dad, stop using all those F-words.'

The expression on the faces of his new flock suddenly made him lost for words.


# A Drink For the Road

Most vicarages receive visits from gentlemen of the road. The normal policy is to provide such visitors with a mug of tea and a sandwich. Several vicarages keep a mug in the kitchen for this purpose. On this day the vicar and his wife were out on visits and their teenage daughter was at home alone.

The doorbell rang and the girl went to answer it. She was greeted by the sight of a young man with long hair, a beard and scruffy clothes. Recognizing the type, she said, 'Just a moment,' and closed the door.

Dutifully, she went off to the kitchen where she made a cup of tea (with the regulation milk and two sugars) and a jam sandwich. She then presented these to the caller, saying, 'Just leave the cup on the doorstep when you are finished,' and closed the door in his face.

A few moments later the doorbell rang again. The girl returned to the visitor.

'Excuse me,' he said. 'There seems to be some mistake. I have an appointment with your father. I'm the new diocesan youth officer...'

# CHAPTER 2

# Services That Go Wrong

## Bringing the House Down

It was the vicar's first Christmas in his new church and the congregation were being most welcoming. Keen to make a good start and to show his appetite for a party, he was not averse to having the odd glass of mulled wine.

He left the churchwarden's party a little earlier than the others because he suddenly remembered that he was doing the Christmas Eve service, in the curate's absence. Worrying at his lack of sermon preparation, he came up with a cunning plan of keeping the congregation entertained.

However, the service started to go wrong with the introduction of the christingles. One young boy, excited by what mischief he could cause with the candle on the christingle, decided that it would be good fun to set something on fire. Unfortunately, the target was the unsuspecting vicar, who, as he turned round from helping to light another child's christingle, smelt that something was burning and was perplexed to find that it was his cassock that was alight. Heroically, he managed to retain his calm expression despite this interruption.

After this commotion he tried to continue with the service, but this flirtation with fire should have been a warning. His cunning plan for the sermon to keep the congregation amused was to set off some household fireworks to represent the star in the sky hoping that it would stimulate the same awe in his congregation as it did to the original shepherds in the field.

What he was not to realize was that his wife, wishing to tidy the house, had put all the fireworks together in the same box. He proceeded to light what he thought would just be a small banger with some sparks, but to his surprise the firework took off and crashed into the roof of the 600-year-old church.

As masonry began falling from the ceiling, his mind slightly slowed by the tipple of wine, he remained in his pulpit proclaiming that this was a sign from God while

the congregation rushed out of the church as rubble
continued to crash to the ground.

# I Do?

A vicar was taking the wedding service of a noble, upright
family from the parish. However, he was taken aback
when he asked if anyone had 'just cause or reason' to
prohibit the marriage going ahead. He was surprised,
because he heard the words 'I do'. What shocked him
more was the fact that the person lodging the complaint
was the bride's father.

It turned out that the poor old chap was profoundly
deaf, and he had arranged with the vicar previously
that when he was asked 'who is giving this woman to be
married', the vicar would look at him. That would be his
cue to say 'I do'. However, the vicar looked up slightly
too early and found the man objecting to his daughter's
happy day.

# Out of Tune

An organist was engaged by a firm of undertakers to
play the organ at a funeral at the local crematorium.
The hymn that had been requested by the family of the
deceased was 'Do not be afraid'. The undertakers told the
organist that as it was not in the service book it would be
printed on a separate sheet. So the organist looked up
the hymn and did a double-take when he read the words.

He called into the funeral director's office when he visited town later that day and showed him the words of the hymn. He shared his opinion about the words and decided it would be best to omit the offending verse.

They discussed alerting the priest taking the funeral about their decision, because he was making the copies for the service. When they failed to reach him on the phone, they decided that as he was a perceptive chap he would spot the problem himself.

The day of the funeral arrived and when the priest arrived at the crematorium the organist said: 'I suppose you have left out the second verse of "Do not be afraid"?'

'No,' the priest replied. 'Why should I have done?'

The organist then pointed out the words of the second verse. At the door of the crematorium chapel afterwards, not one mourner commented on the choice of hymn, nor did anyone mention the verse which had read:

When the fire is burning all around you,
You will never be consumed by the flames...

## You're Sitting In My Seat

The long procession began to make its way down the aisle of the church, which was packed with parishioners and local dignitaries, together with the friends and family of the priest who was to be inducted and installed. Led by the crucifer and the choir, the double line of robed figures slowly passed the Archdeacon and the Bishop, who were waiting at the west end of the nave. Last of all was the Bishop's chaplain. Often, the climax of an ecclesiastical procession is the last member, but not so when the Bishop is accompanied by his chaplain, who must creep anonymously behind him.

Throughout the opening ceremonies, the Bishop's chaplain juggled with the Bishop's crozier, mitre, order of service and hymn-sheet, as discreetly as possible.

Fortunately for his peace of mind, he didn't know until afterwards (when he was informed by a helpful busy-body), that the particular way he held the crozier signified that the Bishop had died. In blissful ignorance of this nicety of posture, he thought he was doing quite well.

Suddenly, everyone knelt. At first, it seemed to the chaplain that he would have to remain standing, having nowhere to kneel. Then he noticed an empty stall nearby, presumably kept for him. Thankfully and, as he thought, invisibly, he lowered himself in it, while the crozier still proclaimed, to those of the congregation who knew of such things, that the Bishop was not as well as he looked.

The chaplain's tranquillity was short-lived. Glancing up, he saw advancing upon him the Archdeacon with the new incumbent, whom he was about to install in the place mistakenly occupied by the now all-too-visible chaplain.

## Marital Problems

A priest had seen a young couple grow up in his parish and was delighted when they announced they were getting married. He even helped them through part of their marriage preparation, but as he was appointed to a new post, he was not able to continue this.

The couple still wanted the priest to take part in the service, so they wrote to him and invited him to marry them in his old church, but due to other commitments he was not able to attend.

Instead he decided to send the couple a telegram to wish them well on their wedding day. Down at the Post Office he diligently wrote out the message, which was to include a Bible verse.

The verse he wanted to share with the couple was 1 John 4:18: 'There is no fear in love, but perfect love casts out fear.'

However the operator missed out the first '1' and sent instead the reference John 4:18: 'The fact is, you have had five husbands, and the man you now have is not your husband.'

# Hair-Raising Sermon

The preacher mounted the pulpit for his sermon, and as the hymn ended, he invited the congregation to be seated for the prayer.

An elderly gentleman in the front row of the gallery bowed his head a little too vigorously and his wig fell off, landing on the lap of a lady seated on the floor below.

Opening her eyes with a start, she looked around to see where this homeless hairpiece had come from. As she looked around she noticed a bald man sitting in front of her, and hoping to spare the poor man's blushes she crammed the wig on to the man's head and then quickly bowed her head and shut her eyes.

Managing with difficulty to contain himself, the preacher finished his prayer, wondering what the recipient's wife would think when she opened her eyes to discover that her husband had miraculously grown a new head of hair.

## Name This Child...

It was a particularly busy time of the year for this con-
scientious minister, who normally took a great deal of
time with all of his parishioners, regardless of their need.

A couple on the fringe of the church had asked him
several months before if he would baptize their baby when
it was born. He knew the wife very well, and agreed to
the request, but told her that they would go through all
the details much nearer the time.

However, what with a host of other requirements on
his time he found that the day of the baptism had come
around. With little time beforehand for rehearsals and so
on, he had to make do with chatting through the arrange-
ments with the couple on the phone the night before.

The next morning they all assembled at the church for the service and the vicar took the child in his arms to perform the baptism. At that point he realized that he had forgotten to check on the child's name.

'What are you calling the child?' he asked the parents.

'Simon Homer,' replied the father.

Surprised at this choice of name, the vicar said to him, 'Is Homer your favourite poet?'

The father looked at him strangely. 'Poet? No!'

'Well, why have you chosen this name?'

'Because I keep pigeons,' said the father.

# Body Double

A young vicar was preparing to take his first funeral and he knew that it was going to be an emotional experience because the deceased, a Mr John Smith, was one of the most respected members of the parish.

The nervous young man had prepared himself for the event and despite his trepidation was quietly confident that things would go well. Sadly, he was mistaken.

The first problem arose when the funeral cortege arrived at the cemetery. Situated on the outskirts of town, the place of rest was an oasis of quiet ... apart from the garage which was doing a roaring trade with its cut-price petrol. In fact, it was so popular that the procession of funeral cars had some bother getting through the queue for petrol.

After a short delay they eventually managed to get everyone to the grave, and the vicar was quickly called upon to calm the widow, who was getting quite agitated that her husband's funeral, which she had hoped would be a solemn and respectful occasion, was not going to plan.

Having settled her, the vicar moved on and, amidst the sounds of banging and engines revving managed to conduct the service.

Following the interment of the body, he was just breathing a sigh of relief that it had all gone so well when a voice called out over the garage tannoy: 'Will John Smith please come to the body shop.'

At that the widow finally broke down in floods of tears.

## An Offering For the Sick

The Sunday morning service had just got under way when the vicar noticed that one of the young mums in the congregation was having trouble with one of her children.

What the vicar did not hear was the child fidgeting and complaining. 'I'm feeling sick,' the little girl said. The mother gave her a mint imperial and told her to take deep breaths, thinking that the ill-feeling was probably due to the child's over-indulgence of chocolate.

However, as the service progressed the little girl's discomfort increased and for the sake of peace in a quiet time of worship, the mother told her daughter to go outside where she could be sick in the garden. 'Then you will feel much better,' she said.

The little girl made her way quietly out of the church and the time of worship continued undisturbed.

A few minutes later the little girl returned and her mother inquired if she did now feel better.

35

'Yes, I was sick, but there was a box at the back of the church that said "For the sick", so I was sick in that.'

## Revelations

An ordained friend was once asked to officiate at an adult baptism service. As is often the case, he was required first to conduct the service of immersion and afterwards to preach.

Arriving at the service he conducted the baptism and then was given plenty of time to change from his wet clothes into his preacher's suit. Towelling himself down in the vestry he discovered to his horror that his under-pants were missing.

He felt sure that he had placed them somewhere safe before the service, but although he searched high and low they were not to be found. Unable to bring himself to put on his suit trousers without underwear, he contrived to dry his swimming trunks as adequately as possible and put them on under his suit.

Returning to the service he took his stand in full view of the congregation and began to preach the sermon. The evening being rather warm and the preacher's sermon being rather long, the moisture retained in his swimming costume began to seep through into the fabric of his trousers.

As his predicament became increasingly clear he became more and more uncomfortable, knowing that the congregation were looking at the damp patch showing up on his trousers. As he struggled on, his discomfort only led to him sweating profusely.

Pausing to mop his fevered brow, he reached into the top pocket of his jacket for his handkerchief only to pro-duce, in full view of the congregation, a large pair of multi-coloured Y-fronts.

## They're Playing Our Song

A young couple were looking forward to their wedding day and they both wanted to incorporate a song that meant a great deal to them in the service. They asked the vicar if it would be possible to have played on the organ the song 'Everything I do, I do for you', which was featured in the Kevin Costner film of *Robin Hood: Prince of Thieves*.

They were delighted when the vicar said that would be no problem. 'Just tell the organist what you want,' he told them. When they spoke to the organist, who was of a certain age, he mumbled under his breath, but assured them that he knew the song and would play it.

On the happy day all went well until the couple turned at the end of the service to march out of church. To their horror, the old organist was playing the 1950s TV theme tune: 'Robin Hood, Robin Hood, riding through the glen ...' The look on the faces of the newly-weds was reportedly caught on video for posterity...

## Out Of the Mouths...

A vicar was in the middle of taking the wedding service of an older couple from his parish when he began to get the impression that something was not quite right, even though the congregation was in place, the day was sunny enough, and the music melodious. No, the trouble seemed to be in front of him, coming from the bridal party.

The groom was fidgety and unsettled, but the clergy-man was not in a position to find out immediately what was wrong. The bride was seen to be muttering when the best man suddenly turned and walked out of the church.

The priest was perplexed. Thankfully, a hymn was approaching and he decided he would inquire of the couple as to their problem once the congregation started singing.

However, he had only got to the point of announcing the number of the hymn when the best man rushed back in to the church and handed a box to the groom.

'Ah, that's it,' thought the vicar, 'they have forgotten the wedding rings.'

He was taken aback to see the groom open the box, pull out a pair of false teeth and slip them into his mouth, just in time to say 'I will'.

# CHAPTER 3

# All Abroad – Travellers' Tales

## To Catch a Thief...

One day a missionary in Africa had her necklace stolen. She asked all who worked in her area if they had seen it, but all denied any knowledge. She was, however, sure that one of the locals had taken it.

In desperation to get back her piece of jewellery, which had more sentimental value than anything else, she went to the village chief and explained the situation. Was there anything he could do to help?

The chief said there was. Just leave the matter with him, and if the necklace had been stolen he would get it back, he assured her.

At that she became a little anxious. She did not want anyone to be harmed and she had visions of harsh punishments being meted out to the culprit.

The village chief called in the three main suspects. He explained to them about the missionary's loss and he asked them if they had taken the necklace. They all denied it. He then handed each of the men a handful of rice and asked them to chew it.

The missionary wondered what would happen next.

Then, after a few moments, he asked the men to spit out the rice. The chief looked at each man's rice and pointed to one of the men, who instantly confessed and pleaded for forgiveness.

Afterwards, the missionary asked the chief how he had worked out from the rice who the thief was.

'That was easy,' he said. 'You see, the guilty man was nervous and could not produce as much saliva as the others, so his rice was the hardest.'

# Best Foot Forward

A missionary in Africa was well respected by the locals, not only because of his upstanding life-style and clear preaching of the gospel, but also because he was supremely talented and could fix almost anything.

In this part of Africa, communications with the home-land were very difficult, and members of his home church tried to help out by sending various supplies. One little old lady had a deep distrust of the postal service and she came up with a cunning plan to beat the postal workers who might try to steal her packages.

Her plan was to send two pairs of shoes, but to send one package with two left shoes and the right shoes in the second package. Her plan would have worked well, but the postal system proved sadly lacking. In the event only one package arrived. The missionary received the package, but put the two left shoes to one side feeling that there was little he could do with them.

One of the locals saw these, however, and asked if he could take them. They were shiny and new, the sort of thing that he rarely saw. He proudly set off with his new possessions to show them off to his neighbours.

A few hours later he returned to the missionary's house. Would it be possible, he wondered, taking into account the missionary's handiwork skills, to do something to one of the shoes to make it right-footed?

# Impressive Visitor

When the Archbishop of Canterbury visited Fiji some years ago, a friend of a friend who was a schoolteacher there, was feeling very proud to be an Anglican.

The lunchtime communion service in Suva Cathedral welcomed the Archbishop with all the pomp it could muster, and he brought his own splendour to the occasion. After the service there was a bring-and-share lunch, and it brought a lump to the throat to see the head of the worldwide Anglican communion modestly peeling a banana and talking to members of the congregation during the rather basic lunch, which must have been a great contrast to the state banquets and official dinners he was used to.

The teacher was thrilled to be permitted to take some of the senior students to the cathedral with her. She thought to herself, this is an event they will never forget, something to tell their grandchildren about.

At last it was all over. As they climbed back into the car to return to school, the teacher was thinking deep thoughts about the church breaking down all barriers of time, race, culture, etc., and said to the students: 'Wasn't that wonderful?'

One of the teenagers settled back into her seat with a wide grin on her face. 'Great. We missed double maths.'

## Dog-gone Visitors

An Australian friend of a friend who was a missionary to Hong Kong was planning to return to his homeland for a short holiday and in a gesture of Christian hospitality agreed to a request from one of his friends who led another Chinese missionary organization.

His friend told him that close friends of his, a Chinese missionary couple from the mainland, were coming to Hong Kong and were looking for somewhere to stay. The Australian promptly offered the use of his flat for the visitors. They were delighted at the offer and as he left for Australia, the couple arrived to take up residence.

A few weeks later he returned to find that they had left his home in pristine condition. Everything was in its place and it even looked cleaner than when he had left it.

However, one thing worried him. He couldn't find his pet dog. He inquired of all the neighbours; none had seen his pet. He put up notices on street lights near his home. He even offered a reward.

Puzzled at this mysterious disappearance, he mentioned it to his mission friend. 'Ah, yes, that was a problem,' he mumbled.

It transpired that the Chinese couple had arrived at the flat and had interpreted the presence of the dog as a gift from the owner to them. They had been overjoyed at this thoughtful gesture and had enjoyed a tasty canine meal, quite unaware they were scoffing their absent host's pet.

The poor man was inconsolable for weeks.

# Card Trick

A missionary who had just arrived in a remote part of Africa was constantly amazed at the relaxed attitude of the locals to modern life. They seemed quite free from the stresses that plagued people back home.

Often, the locals would sit around drinking tea or chatting or playing card games. One of the games caught the attention of the missionary. He watched people playing it but despite all of his best intellectual efforts, the rules of this game eluded him. The players would turn up cards in front of each player and then sit there watching them, sometimes for as long as 15 minutes. Then, suddenly, someone would be declared a winner.

The missionary eventually gave up and asked the players what they were playing at.

'The rules are simple,' he was told, 'the winner is the person whose card the first fly lands on.'

## In Sickness and In Health

A missionary doctor working in the jungles of Asia was very pleased at the success rate at their small, remote hospital. The recovery record was one that many bigger hospitals would have been proud of, but one day things began to go wrong.

One of the patients who was on a life support machine inexplicably died. Now, while this was a tragedy, such outcomes were not unheard of in hospitals. What concerned the doctor was that this was the third time in just a few months that a patient, who appeared to be on the mend, suddenly took a turn for the worse and expired.

The doctor mentioned this to his colleagues, and a nurse said she thought it was suspicious that all the patients that had died had done so on the same bed. Her theory, that the bed was 'jinxed', was dismissed out of hand.

A few days later, the doctors were stunned to find
that a fourth patient had inexplicably and suddenly died
– again, in the same bed. An emergency meeting was called
and after all the patient records were examined no reasonable explanation could be found for the poor man's
early demise. The medical staff decided that they would
now monitor the bed to see if there was any interference
with the equipment.

They didn't have long to wait. The next morning a
staff member watched in amazement as one of the cleaners
came into the ward and nonchalantly pulled out the
plug of the life-support machine in order to plug in her
floor polisher.

# CHAPTER 4

# The Learning Process

## Exam Nerves

A student at a theological college had been pursuing a very successful course, but when he came to sit one of the exams he was suddenly shaken by an extreme and unusual attack of nerves. Looking at the exam paper in front of him, his mind went a complete blank and nothing made sense, so much so that he could not begin to think of a way to answer the questions.

Looking around, he was irritated to see his fellow students setting-to and obviously relishing the challenge that faced them. He looked again at his paper and it might as well have been written in Russian for all he could make of it.

A resourceful man, however, he decided that he would cut his losses and compose a letter to his mother in the exercise book provided for the answers. At the end of the examination he picked up his books and handed the invigilator one of his exercise books. He then hurriedly left the hall and went back to his room where he consulted his text books and wrote out the answers to the questions in the exam. He then found an envelope which he addressed to his mother, inserted the exercise book and put it in the post box.

The next day he was summoned by the college principal to explain why he handed in a letter to his mother instead of the answers to the exam questions. He explained that he had written the letter in one book and the answers in another. The two books must have got mixed up, he said. The principal called up the mother of the student and asked her to post back the envelope from the college straightaway.

A few days later the principal was satisfied with the student's explanation when he received the envelope, unopened, postmarked the day of the exam. He got top marks.

## Caught Out

Two students at a theological college had worked hard throughout their long course. They had done well in all their exams and both had proved popular with staff and students alike. As their finals approached, neither was particularly concerned about the testing time ahead.

The weekend before the last of their exams they were both invited to a friend's birthday party, which was being celebrated at the other end of the country. They decided that they would take time out of their studies to go and help celebrate.

The party was a huge success, almost as huge as the hangover both were nursing the following morning. Over some strong black coffee, they decided that it would be quite reasonable to take the day off. They anticipated that as they knew their course tutor well, they would simply explain to him that they had suffered a flat tyre on the return journey and had missed the exam. They felt sure that he would take pity on them and allow them to sit the exam separately from their fellow students.

With the plan carefully worked out, they took their time returning to college. When they got back, they sought out their tutor and told him their story. They were pleasantly surprised when he willingly agreed to them sitting the exam the following day. The only condition was that they would have to be in separate rooms.

The next day they settled down with their exam papers. The first question was easy enough: 'Assess the arguments for the authorship of Isaiah. (5 points)'

Then they turned to the second and final question: 'Which tyre? (95 points)'

## Teacher Training

A group of theology students who were studying church history found the lecturer, and the subject, rather boring. They had no choice but to attend the class, but as their interest dwindled they began to test how interested the lecturer was in them.

They began by gradually moving their desks, inch by inch, eventually ending up (after several weeks) in different positions to where they started. The students who started the lectures at the back of the class had moved their desks to the front, and so on, with no comment from their lecturer. They did this each week during his lecture throughout the course.

They hatched a plan to try to 'train' the lecturer, in the way that Pavlov trained his dogs.

What they did was to feign a lack of interest, only showing interest when the lecturer moved towards the waste paper basket. To their astonishment, the lecturer responded to their reaction. After a few weeks he lectured only when he was standing next to the bin.

They decided to push their experiment even further. So over the next few months they succeeded in 'training' the lecturer to the extent that by the end of the academic year they had 'trained' him to deliver his talks standing on top of the waste paper basket.

All of the students graduated from the class with straight 'A's.

# Rapturous Reception

A new student arrived at a theological college and proved to be extremely keen to learn. He was also keen to impart his knowledge to his fellow students, which wasn't a problem at first.

Unfortunately, he was a self-appointed expert on the Book of Revelation and had clear views on the Rapture. He insisted on sharing his views on these subjects at every opportunity, frequently pointing out major world events and how these were echoed in the New Testament.

His room mates were especially unhappy, as they had nowhere to go to escape his rantings. He would even identify world leaders and which ones might be the Anti-Christ. After a few weeks this got too much for his fellow students and they decided to get their revenge on him.

One night they got together and hatched a plan that they thought would finally silence him on this subject.

In the middle of the night all of the students in the hall got up and, in complete silence, made their way to the attic. When they were all safely assembled, one of their number, a keen musician, was dispatched downstairs where he produced a trumpet and blew it for all he was worth.

The hapless student woke to find himself seemingly alone in the building, having just heard the trumpet of which he was all too aware. After that he rarely referred to the Book of Revelation again...

# CHAPTER 5

# Parishioner Problems

## House Meeting

The lady who ran the women's group in the local church was due to host a meeting of the ladies from the local council of churches, but because she had to collect her husband from the airport earlier that day she warned them that she might be a little late for the meeting which was to take place at her house.

On the day, a group of four women from one church arrived at the gate to find two other women on the door-step, ringing the bell. The door was opened and all six women were shepherded into the living room. A few moments later the doorbell rang again and several more women arrived. The ladies made themselves at home in the living room, enjoying the warmth of the real fire as it had been a rather chilly day outside.

As they sat down the phone rang and it was answered by the lady who had answered the door. Later she came in and said, 'I don't know how to tell you this...'

The others expected her to say that the hostess was probably still at the airport, and the secretary of the group was about to say that they should start the meeting anyway, when the lady told them, 'No, the plane isn't delayed, but I think you are in the wrong house.'

It turned out that a typing error had replaced 'Avenue' with 'Road' and a dozen ladies had settled themselves in the home of a stranger.

The secretary asked the lady, 'Why did you let us all in?'

'Well,' she replied, 'I saw my daughter's friend at the door with a woman I took to be her mum. And then I thought her mum must have lots of friends.'

# Interpreting Moses

A Sunday school class of eight- and nine-year-olds had been learning about the life and deeds of Moses. One Sunday the teacher asked the children to draw a picture to illustrate one of the lessons they had been taught.

Pictures were produced of Moses in the bulrushes, Moses and the burning bush, Moses and the various plagues on the people of Egypt, Moses and the people crossing the Red Sea and Moses and the Ten Commandments. These delighted the teacher who was gratified to see that her efforts at teaching these Bible stories had been successful. All of the paintings were recognized and the children were complimented on their work.

But one child had produced a picture which the teacher couldn't understand. The child had drawn a picture of an aeroplane full of people. The teacher asked what part of the life of Moses the picture was supposed to represent.

'The flight out of Egypt,' came the reply.

The teacher responded: 'So I suppose the person up the front is Moses?'

'Oh no,' came the reply, 'that's Pontius the pilot!'

# Holy Spirits

In a pub a quiz night was taking place. A friend was taking part and was delighted to secure joint first place. The organizers decided that they would need to have a winner, so a further question was produced. There was delight on his face when the tie-break question was read out: 'Who is the Primate of England?'

With the benefit of his extensive and detailed knowledge of the Church of England, he confidently wrote down the answer: The Archbishop of York.

To his dismay he was told that the answer was the Archbishop of Canterbury. He expressed his disgust to the manager and offered to produce the *Church of England Yearbook* to prove that the Primate of All England is the Archbishop of Canterbury, while the Primate of England is indeed the Archbishop of York.

Such a worthy tome was not sufficient for the landlord: 'It says here that the answer is the Archbishop of Canterbury. And this is from the brewery!'

## Finders Keepers

A lady of the parish was on her way home one evening, enjoying a quiet drive when she spotted out of the corner of her eye something glinting on the roadside.

She pulled up and got out of her car to investigate. She was rather puzzled to find what certainly looked like a microwave oven. While it was slightly different to those she had seen before she was sure that it would do the business in her kitchen, even if the badge on it was not one she recognized.

Looking around, she decided that someone must have thrown it away. Striking while the iron was hot, she man-handled the machine into her car and set off, feeling rather pleased with herself.

She had only gone a few yards when she saw a blue flashing light behind her. She pulled over and guessing the officers of the law must have seen her stealing the oven, she resolved to come clean and confess.

'I'm sorry, officer,' she said as she stepped out of the car. 'I just saw it lying there and thought I could cook some nice meals for my family.'

'Oh yes,' said one of the policemen. 'I don't think you would have cooked much with our radar speed trap, madam.'

# I'll Name That Tune...

A friend of a friend who worked for a radio production company had an idea for a radio programme that he thought would go down well on a Christian radio station. He heard of a station in America that sounded a likely candidate and wrote off suggesting his idea for the programme.

He was delighted when they wrote back saying that they were interested. Would he do a pilot programme, they asked. To comply with the station's rules, he would have to fill in a form listing all the music and contribu- tors. It was their policy only to feature Christians, they said.

This did not seem too onerous, so he put the pro- gramme together, together with some nice classical music. He duly sent off the tape and waited to hear what recep- tion his programme would receive.

He was stunned a few weeks later to get his tape back, together with a letter stating that the station could not possibly use the programme, for he had included

'Finlandia' by Sibelius as the theme tune. As this was a secular song, they could not broadcast it. However, if he changed the theme song to a Christian tune, the programme would fit in very well with their schedules.

The budding producer took the form, scored out the song and replaced it with 'The Day Thou Gavest', but he didn't tell the station that the hymn's tune was 'Finlandia' by Sibelius. Ignorant of that detail, the programme was proudly featured on their schedules.

# Christmas Chaos

A friend of a friend worked for a large multinational company. One year he was invited to visit his company's headquarters in Japan, combining a fact-finding mission with helping to bolster relationships with the company's directors both there and in this country.

On arriving in Tokyo the first few days went very well. He was shown around the company's magnificent building and he even got to see some of the main tourist attractions in what was to him a very foreign country.

On the last day of his trip, his hosts suggested they take him Christmas shopping. He found the experience illuminating, for as it was December he was struck by the way that Japanese stores had adopted Christmas themes to help boost festive trade.

Being a keen Christian, he found this a good way to initiate a conversation with his host on the differences between the Shinto religion and his own faith. He took advantage of the nativity scenes in the shop windows to share his faith with his host.

This proved to be a rewarding experience for his host was a very religious man himself and was deeply committed to his Shinto faith. He drank in the explanations offered from his British visitor. He was equally delighted to have the store decorations as visual aids to the lecture on the Christian faith. However the British Christian was quite taken aback, and momentarily silenced, on visiting one store where he saw a gleaming nativity scene, complete with a toy Santa Claus nailed to a cross...

# A Lifting Experience

Two ladies from a remote parish in the north were delighted to be invited to a church conference in Los Angeles. Not only would they get to see the movie capital of the world, but they would have the chance to hear some inspiring Christian speakers, and the journey would be subsidized by their parish.

However, arriving in Los Angeles, they were surprised at how difficult it was to get around, as there was little public transport and everyone warned them to take care as the city had a violent reputation.

One of the two took fright and spent the entire week in the hotel, which was hosting the conference. She did not venture outside for anything, and they got to the end of their holiday with her friend feeling a little cheated out of sightseeing opportunities.

On the last night she succeeded in talking her friend into accompanying her on a night time tour of the city. The two ladies put on their best clothes and got into the lift as they set out to see the city.

After getting into the lift, the ladies were rather perplexed when it stopped at the next floor and a gruff muscle-bound, black, man with a large Doberman got into the lift with them. From behind his dark glasses he turned to the women and said: 'Hit the ground!' They dived to the floor and pleaded with him not to hurt them.

'No, I meant "hit the ground floor button", ' he said, laughing.

The next morning they were still laughing at their experience over breakfast. As they went to pay the bill for their hotel room, the receptionist told them that their bill had been settled the night before by a Mr Eddie Murphy.

## What's In a Name?

An active Anglican had decided to improve the status
of his learning by taking a counselling course at St John's
College in Nottingham. While the course was mainly
completed by correspondence, there were three resi-
dential periods spent at the college.

The student valued his time at the college greatly,
and when it was celebrating its 25th anniversary, he
along with many others was invited to join in the
festivities.

When he arrived at the campus he found that there
were several hundred people in attendance, and a huge
marquee had been erected, equipped with seating and
platform for the speakers. The guest of honour was to

be Archbishop George Carey, who was to preach at a celebration Eucharist.

The morning session broke for lunch and people took the opportunity to renew acquaintances with former friends and colleagues. Our friend wandered off around the college and in a corridor near the library he saw the Archbishop approaching. Dr Carey looked at him and said, 'Hello, Ted.'

Our friend stopped in his tracks. He, of course, knew the Archbishop, but how, he wondered, did the Archbishop know him? He cast his mind back trying to recall what wonderful meeting he had forgotten and was marvelling at Dr Carey's ability to remember names when he noticed that he was wearing a rather large lapel badge with the name 'Ted' on it.

## Holiday Horror

A family set off on their caravan holiday to France – father, mother, two children and granny. As they approached the ferry terminal at Dover the father jokingly said, 'I hope everyone's got their passport ready.'

The granny piped up: 'No, I didn't think you needed a passport for France.'

It was too late to turn back and get the missing document, so the father came up with an alternative plan. 'What we will do is this. Granny can hide in the caravan until we get to the other side. On the way back we will just say that the passport has been stolen.' Satisfied with this plan, they set off and crossed over into France with no questions asked.

On landing on the French side they carried on until they reached the first service station where they all got out to stretch their weary legs. However, on opening the caravan they discovered to their horror that granny had died on the crossing.

'What are we going to do now, we have a dead relative in a foreign country and no documents for her?' said the wife.

The father said he would call the British embassy for advice. He was pleasantly surprised by what he heard.

'Don't worry,' said the official. 'We have had this problem before. What you must do is get back in the car and drive straight to the embassy compound. Once you are inside we can deal with the formalities, but it is important you come straight here.'

Relieved, the family had a coffee to settle their strained nerves. However on returning to the car park they found the car and caravan had been stolen...

## Just Drive

Two New-Age travellers were returning from their recent protesting at the building of a bypass when they tried to hitch a lift to their home in the West Country.

After a short period standing at the junction of a major road, a lady churchwarden pulled up and they jumped into the car.

Although she didn't look at them, she nevertheless asked where they wanted to go. They named a town, but said that they would be happy to be let off anywhere on this road.

They closed the door and the lady set off. She continued to drive without addressing either of the two young men, refusing to join in any conversation with them.

Eventually they arrived at their destination and the lady stopped the car. As they got out, they both expressed their gratitude. 'Thanks for the lift,' one of the young men said.

'Lift?', she exclaimed, 'I thought you were hijacking my car.'


# No Bugging Here

Many years ago, two Christian businessmen had to go to the USSR for an important meeting. When they arrived in Moscow they were immediately intimidated by the suspicious attitude of the officials they met. They were annoyed that they were herded everywhere and that there was no freedom to discover the mysterious city for themselves.

Worse, they had the impression that their every move was being watched. When they checked into their hotel they found they had been given a rather grand twin room on the first floor. As they began unpacking, one of the men said to the other, 'Do you think the room will be bugged?' After their less than hospitable welcome, they decided to check out the room themselves.

They looked behind curtains, under tables, around lamps and on the back of the paintings on the wall. The room, to their surprise, seemed 'clean'.

But then one of the men pointed to the carpet. Rolling back the magnificent rug they discovered to their horror a small box-like contraption that could only be one thing. Determined to maintain their privacy in the face of the Communist threat, they found a screwdriver and began to dismantle the spying device. The task was not as easy as they assumed. It took both of them nearly a full quarter of an hour to unscrew the bolt and to their joy the 'bug' eventually came off. They were puzzled that, apart from a hole in the bottom of the box, there appeared to be no listening device or wiring.

Satisfied, the two men then changed for dinner and went downstairs to the hotel's restaurant. When they got there they saw a scene of commotion as the room's grand, and very expensive, chandelier had crashed to the floor from its housing – right under their bedroom.

# Father to the Man
*and other stories*

## Adrian Plass

What is a forty-something bloke to do when he and his wife don't seem to talk any more, his teenage son is alienated from him and his best mate – reliable drinking companion for many years – suddenly and inexplicably becomes a Christian?

What do a family do when a much-loved grandparent dies unexpectedly and a freshly baked cake is discovered, obviously intended to be eaten when all were together?

These are just two of the dilemmas to be addressed among many others in this latest collection of stories from the writer who created the Sacred Diarist and *An Alien at St Wilfred's.*

# The Sacred Diary of Adrian Plass aged 45$^3/_4$

*Illustrated by Dan Donovan*

Adrian Plass

Certainly a little older, perhaps just a tiny bit wiser, Adrian Plass was amazed when his account of 'serious spiritual experiences' in *The Sacred Diary of Adrian Plass aged 37¾* became widely read and appreciated as a funny book! More books have followed and now he's in demand as a public speaker all over the place. As we follow him to a variety of venues the reason why Christian speakers need travelling mercies becomes abundantly clear!

Many of the characters we met in the first *Sacred Diary* are with us again – Leonard Thynn, the Flushpools, Gerald (grown up now, of course!), Adrian's wife Anne, voluptuous Gloria Marsh, Edwin (the wise church elder) and the ever-religious Richard and Doreen Cook – as well as one or two new characters; Stephanie Widgeon, for instance, who only seems to have one thing to say...

One last question – what is a banner ripping seminar?

# Stress Family Robinson

## Adrian Plass

The Robinson family – mother, father, two teenage sons and a six-year-old daughter who is everybody's favourite – are a typical Christian family – or are they?

Does life behind the front door of the tall, thin Victorian semi-detached where they live match up to (or even resemble) the image they convey at their parish church?

The one person who knows the Robinsons almost better than they know themselves is dear Dip Reynolds – trusted friend-extraordinaire who has a few surprising secrets of her own to reveal...

# Adrian Plass Classics
*The Growing Up Pains of Adrian Plass*
*View from a Bouncy Castle*
*Cabbages for the King*

Adrian Plass

Adrian Plass's unique perspective on life and faith can be enjoyed once more in this omnibus edition of three of his best-selling books. In *The Growing Up Pains of Adrian Plass*, we meet the real Adrian Plass, as opposed to his fictional counterpart in the *Sacred Diary* series. *Cabbages for the King* and *View from a Bouncy Castle* are collections of stories, sketches and poems which celebrate both the profundity and the absurdity of life, while making keen points about the gospel. Underlying Adrian's irrepressible humour is his passionate conviction that God embraces us in our weakness and vulnerability, and that we need to gain a child-like perspective in order to understand just how much he loves us.

# An Alien at St Wilfred's

Adrian Plass

- Who wants to poison the organist?

- Why is the overhead projector so very annoyed?

- Who made the vicar burst into tears in his own pulpit?

- What on earth is happening to the church lighting?

- Why did four sane Anglicans meet on top of the tower in a raging storm?

- What is going on?

It's very simple – there's an alien at St Wilfred's!

This is the story of Nunc, the small alien, who comes to Earth and learns to speak Prayer Book English – all told in the inimitable style of best-selling author Adrian Plass.